98.6 MEDITATIONS
To Maintain Spiritual Well-Being

98.6 MEDITATIONS

To Maintain Spiritual Well-Being

by Francis P. LeBuffe, S.J.

Edited by Catherine Hughes
and Anne Taylor

ARENA LETTRES—WALDWICK, NEW JERSEY

Original edition published in 1949 by the Apostleship of Prayer

Imprimi potest: John J. McMahon, S.J.

Nihil obstat: John M. A. Fearns, S.T.D.
Censor Librorum

Imprimatur: Francis Cardinal Spellman, D.D.
Archbishop of New York

Library of Congress Catalog Card Number: 84-071932

ISBN: 0-88479-041-X

Printed in the United States of America

Designed by Joe Sowinski

CONTENTS

98.6 MEDITATIONS
To Maintain Spiritual Well-Being

KNOWING MY FRIEND

May you have more and more grace and peace
as you come to know our Lord more and more.
2 PETER 1:2

Jesus, dearest Lord, how pleasant a privilege meditation shows itself to be. It is all a study of Your own dear self, a seeking to know You better that I may love You more and follow You more closely. From earlier years I have been taught the lessons of Your life and yet I have a great deal to learn about Your own dear self. So teach me to love that day when You come to call me home. Then I shall see You face to face to know You well throughout eternity. Then, indeed, shall grace and peace be accomplished abidingly within my heart.

REAL TRUSTFULNESS IN GOD

Your strength does not lie in numbers, nor your might in violent men; since you are the God of the humble, the help of the oppressed, the support of the weak, the refuge of the forsaken, the savior of the despairing.

JUDITH 9:11

Dear Lord, after all the mercy You have shown us in the New Law of love, far more than Judith should I have complete trust in You, even when life is darkest. She had never knelt at Your crib, nor listened to You on Galilee's shore, nor stood beneath the cross whereon Your love for us caused You to die. Yet she trusted You absolutely in her life's darkest hour. Shame on me, Lord, that my trust has been so weak. Shame on me to place any limits on Your helping me. I'll try to be more trustful, dear Lord; yes, and most trustful then, when everything seems hopeless.

THEN CAME A DOUBT!

Jesus Christ is the same today as he was yesterday and as he will be forever.

HEBREWS 13:8-9

Dear Lord Jesus, only You can realize what the unchangeableness of Your love means to me. Human friends have often failed me, even when I have needed them most. There is no one, even those I know and who know me best, who can reach into the deepest recesses of my soul. I thank You from my heart for all Your love and I beg You never to let me lose the strong conviction that I now have that despite my ups and downs, despite all my weaknesses and my sins, You are and always will be my changeless Friend.

ONE WHO UNDERSTANDS

Yahweh searches every heart, and knows every plan it devises.

1 CHRONICLES 28:9

O Jesus, changeless Friend, how can I thank You for Your friendship? I do need someone to read my life aright and solve therein all that puzzles me so sorely at times. There is none among men to do this, though they may try with gentlest kindliness to give me aid. And so, dear Lord, it is good, so very good, to know that I can come to You and tell You all—all the great things of life and all the little things, too—and best of all, to know that You will always "understand."

MAKING CHRIST KNOWN

On the following day as John stood there again with two of his disciples, Jesus passed, and John stared hard at him and said, "Look, there is the Lamb of God." Hearing this, the two disciples followed Jesus.

JOHN 1:35-37

Jesus, Friend where others fail, Friend where others cannot help, would I could tell all men the story of Your gentle ways, and bring them, one and all, to love You in return. But that, alas, is an idle wish. Yet some there are with whom I live my shortening days, some whom I have with me at home and some whom I shall meet in the busy ways of life. These at least will I teach the gladness of Your friendship, these few at least will I bring to know Your priceless love and all Your blessed gifts. O Jesus, help me to make You friend to all my friends.

IN LOVE

> God, you are my God, I am seeking you, my soul is thirsting for you, my flesh is longing for you.
>
> PSALMS 63:1

O Jesus, dearest Lord, I love You with my whole heart and with my whole soul, and with my whole mind and with my whole strength and I would love You more. And yet at times You do not share my thoughts as a loved one ought, nor do You steal into every pulse of my searching heart. Oh, no! I have not yet learned to love You as I ought, You are not yet the silent companion of my every moment, whose image buoys my every step. But, Jesus dear, just grant that it may soon be so!

JUST LIKE GOD

Who, God, is comparable to you?
PSALMS 71:19

Dear Jesus, how good You are! Others are kind, but not so kind as You. Others are patient, but none endures what You put up with. Others suffer a bit of neglect and forgetfulness, but none forgives repeated "cuts" as You do. Strangely do I repay Your love; strangely do I try Your patience. Yet You are always my changeless Friend. It's all so wonderful, dear Lord—it's "just like God."

TALKING TO GOD

Lord, teach us to pray.

LUKE 11:1

Dear Jesus, like many another, I, too, have said "I can't pray." Maybe I cannot in any of the higher, loftier forms of prayer because I have not tried very earnestly. But I must not say I cannot talk with You. That would be a very sad admission. Sometimes I talk very freely with You and sometimes, I admit, it is not so easy. But surely I can tell You that much. Sometimes I really don't want to talk with You. But You won't mind, and You will understand if I tell You that, too, quite simply and frankly. Of course You will, for You know my frailty, for You are my changeless Friend.

PET NAMES

You must name him Jesus.

LUKE 1:32

Jesus, there is music in Your sacred name. It is the strongest consolation. No other is so sweet. There is no other that sums up Your love for me—and my love for You. With Bernard, so strong and valiant, I cry out: "Jesus, be Jesus to me!" Be Jesus today and tomorrow and when life begins to wane. Most of all, be Jesus to me throughout the eternal years.

MINDFUL OF GOOD GIFTS

> Remembering Yahweh's achievements, remembering your marvels in the past, I reflect on all that you did, I ponder on all your achievements.
>
> PSALM 77:11-12

Jesus, master of time and of eternity, our days are fast receding into the past. Yet, as we look back over them, we see Your hand stretched out with love over all of them. Here was a gift of nature and there a gift of grace. Here was fresh courage where a moment before had been despair. Thank You, Lord Jesus, for all Your love during those years that are now gone. The memory of those days and weeks and months and years so blessed by You must never die. Grant that they may be alive within my memory forever.

TELL US WHAT YOU SAW

Tell him the meaning of the vision.
DANIEL 8:17

Dear Jesus, thanks to Your own good kindness I have seen the vision, seen God the Father in all his omnipotent majesty, and You, the Son, in Your blessed, winning humanity, and the Holy Ghost in all his compelling love. Mary, too, I have seen and learned to love, as only such a mother can be loved. You have led me up onto the mountian of God and let me look into "the breadth and length and height and depth" of the things of God. To others You have not granted this and they are hungry, very hungry for the vision. So I shall go and try to "tell them all," by word and much more by example. Give me, I beg of You, much grace to tell the vision well.

GOD IS NO KILLJOY

There was a wedding at Cana in Galilee . . . and Jesus and his disciples had also been invited.
JOHN 2:1-2

Dear Jesus, thank You so much for making such a glorious world for my home and for filling it with so much that is beautiful and pleasant. You mean me to enjoy it and for this again I thank You. Only give me grace to enjoy it as You would have me. And if and when I do forego it, in whole or in part, let my motive always be to serve You alone better and more undividedly.

WEARING OUT OUR WELCOME

Do not set foot too often in your neighbour's house, for fear he tires of you and comes to hate you.

PROVERBS 25:17

Dear Lord Jesus, let me always be vividly conscious that I can come to You at any time, in any place, with any thing. I can't do that with earthly friends, no matter how close they are for they have their own troubles and their moods change. But You are my Changeless Friend, "yesterday, today, and the same forever." That should mean everything to me—and it does. So I will come to You lovingly, trustingly, knowing that I shall be welcomed always and that I shall always leave You with joys made holier and sorrows eased. Thank You, dear Lord, for Your changeless love.

THEY DON'T KNOW WHO I AM

Their ways are always under his eye, they cannot be hidden from his sight.
ECCLESIASTICUS 17:15

My God, I am so very glad that You know who I am and will always know, at every moment! Your eyes are upon me and my hidden thoughts and deepest desires are obvious to You. It is so helpful to know this and to realize that You understand me and my frailties and faults, my slight virtues and my occasional attempts at goodness. Let me never weaken in that conviction, but instead grow daily in that happy consciousness. Thank You, Lord, for knowing me.

OUR GROWN-UP FAIRYLAND

> Yahweh God planted a garden in Eden which is in the east, and there he put the man he had fashioned.
>
> GENESIS 2:8

O Jesus, dearest God, I thank You for this fairyland, fairest fairyland of Your own making. Childhood's dreams were very bright; but oh, how poor and mean and frail now that I dwell so really in this, Your land of wonders ever new! Who but You, my God, could have built it all? Who but You could have thought it all? Thanks, thanks for my angel-guides, for my ransomed dead, for the priceless treasures of Your unseen grace! Thanks for Mary, best of mothers, tenderest of queens! Thanks, too, Lord Jesus, for Your own dear hidden self. Please keep me ever in Your fairyland!

GOD EVERYWHERE

> If I climb the heavens, you are there, there too, if I lie in Sheol. If I flew to the point of sunrise, or westward across the sea, your hand would still be guiding me, your right hand holding me.
>
> PSALMS 139:8-10

Dear Jesus, I almost feel like asking whether You Yourself know what it means to have You with me always. But of course You know because You are God and know all things. Yet I must tell You how much it means to me to have You with me always: sanctifying my pleasures and making holy my sorrows, helping me over rough places and with me when I swing merrily along life's path. Dear Jesus, thanks, thanks a thousand times that You are with me everywhere.

DON'T COUNT THE COSTS

What return can I make to Yahweh for all his goodness to me?

PSALMS 116:12

Dear Jesus, no one has done as much for me as You have; and to no one do I owe such a debt of gratitude. To my earthly benefactors I always try to show my thanks. Only in Your regard am I really careless. I am sorry for this, dear Lord, and am quite ashamed of myself. I want to do better in the future and to give all I can to You, for You deserve it, yes, and infinitely more. I promise never again to count the costs.

TARNISHED GIFTS

> When you bring blind animals for sacrifice, is that not wrong? When you bring the lame and the diseased, is that not wrong? Try offering them to your high commissioner, and see if he is pleased with this or receives you graciously, says Yahweh Sabaoth.
>
> MALACHI 1:8

Jesus, patient God, how kind You have been in bearing with my niggardliness! All I have is Your gift, all that I dream of having, if ever it comes to me, will be Your gift, and yet I give so stingily in return. I bear the crosses of life when I see I cannot drop them. I submit to trials and to humiliations only when I see each avenue of escape blocked off. This is so impolite to You, dear Lord, giver of all good gifts, so very ungrateful. Oh, Jesus, give me the grace to give You gifts at least politely!

LONE FIGHTING

He came back to the disciples and found them sleeping, and he said to Peter, "So you had not the strength to keep awake with me one hour?" . . . And he came back again and found them sleeping.

MATTHEW 26:40, 43

Dear Jesus, I am grateful to You for having sought the help of the apostles in Your hours of struggle. I always have a sneaking sense of cowardice when I go to others with my troubles. Yet, I do need help at times and find lone fighting almost impossible. So thank You for Your example; and thank You, too, for those who have aided me when my strength began to fail.

THANKING GOD FOR CROSSES

Go on signing and chanting to the Lord in your hearts, so that always and everywhere you are giving thanks to God who is our Father.
EPHESIANS 5:20

Dear Jesus, let me learn to say "Thank You" for everything that comes to me in life. It is easy to be grateful for what is pleasant and to my liking. But it is hard, very hard, to be at all thankful for pain and disappointments and crosses. You know it; You Yourself found it hard. Yet You were thankful nonetheless. So give me much grace to say "Thank You" for everything.

REPAYING GOD

Is this the return you make to Yahweh? O foolish, unwise people! Is not this your father, who gave you being, who made you, by whom you subsist?
DEUTERONOMY 32:6

Dear Jesus, I have little to pride myself on, when I think of the return I have made to You for all that You have given to me. What shall I return? My best, of course; but even that is poor enough. Yet that is precisely what I have not given. So give me grace now, please, that I may be no longer foolish and senseless, making scant return for all You have lavished on me.

THE SACRAMENT OF PAIN

And thy own soul a sword shall pierce, that out of many hearts thoughts may be revealed.
LUKE 2:51

Dear Jesus, giver of strange gifts, Your gift of pain seems strangest of all. At times I want to grasp its meaning and to realize its sacramental value. At times in my life and in the lives of others, I can almost touch the graces it gives and watch the nearness of our approach to You. And then again at times all grows dark and pain of mind and pain of heart and pain of body seem blighting things that mar man's nature. Yet You would not spoil the comely nature You have made, would You? Then give me in those hours of darkness the grace to receive most holily the sacrament of pain.

MY MOTHER, TOO

Then to the disciple he said, "This is your mother."

JOHN 19:27

O Jesus, my God, I have loved the earthly mother You have given me, loved her in all her goodness, loved her because of all her love for me. And now I shall love my other Mother too, love her with all my heart, with a child's own simple love. She is Yours, but she is mine, too. Like John of old, I shall take her to my own and hold her for my Mother. Thanks, dear Lord Jesus, thanks for Mother Mary. Thanks for all her love these years that are no more. Oh, make me know and love my Mother.

THINKING

She was deeply disturbed by these words and asked herself what this greeting could mean.
LUKE 1:29

Dear Jesus, when shall I learn to face the problems of my life and to steady myself in prudent forethought before I set out upon action? It is hard, of course, at times to stand and neatly poise the balance, but surely it is a thing I must learn soon. "O Wisdom, who has gone forth from the mouth of the Most High, reaching from end to end, strongly yet secretly disposing of things, come and teach us the way of prudence!" For the sake of the prudent Virgin, Your Mother and mine, grant me the peace to think!

GIVING WAY TO GOD

"I am the handmaid of the Lord," said Mary,
"let what you have said be done to me."
LUKE 1:38

Dear Jesus, master of my life and all I have or can ever hope to have, let me learn each hour of the day to kneel beside Your Blessed Mother and yield my will as she did hers. It may be You will come and place what seem to be flat contradictions in my life, as You did in hers; but that is no concern of mine. I am Yours today, tomorrow and tomorrow's morrow. Use me if You will, when You will and as You will. My life is in Your hands.

> Yahweh will come and rest on the whole stretch of Mount Zion and on those who are gathered there, a cloud by day, and smoke, and by night the brightness of a flaring fire. For, over all, the glory of Yahweh will be a canopy and a tent to give shade by day from the heat, refuge and shelter from the storm and rain.
>
> ISAIAH 4:5, 6

Dear Jesus, You have been good enough to teach me much of Your love and to win my love in return. I know You are worthy of the best that is in me and that, try as I may, I can never be worthy of Your love or measure up to Your ideals. But the world is loud in its clamors and the things of the world beckon very appealingly, and at times it is quite difficult to hold my heart from truancy. But I do want to keep the vision bright and I do want to love and serve You always. And so, please never let there be in my eyes dead dreams of You.

MY GOD, I NEED YOU

From the depths I call to you, Yahweh, Lord,
listen to my cry for help!
PSALMS 130:1-2

Dear Jesus, the great consolation in life is to know that I can come to You at any time and any place and in any mood and that You will always understand. That is most consoling to realize when I am all but struck dumb with what life brings. Sometimes it is great happiness that silences me; but mostly the hard things render me numb. But whether I am silent from joy or from sorrow that is when I need You most. And You will understand, won't You, if this is all the prayer I make: "My God, I need You"?

WHEN GOD NEEDS US

If anyone asks you, "Why are you untying it?" you are to say this, "The Master needs it."
LUKE 19:31

Jesus, how is it You have such patience with me? What I ordinarily grant to others, I withhold from You, and dare I make comparison? I readily yield my best to fellowman and when You ask, oh, You know but too well just what I do. You deign to need my help for my own soul and the souls of other men, and now, despite my faithless past, I thank You for this privilege. Let not my past occur again but in the future, by Your grace, may I be ever ready, yes, and ever more eager to give You anything You ask! Let me count it highest privilege to grow weary in serving You!

INTO A DESERT PLACE

Then he said to them, "You must come away to some lonely place all by yourselves and rest for a while"; for there were so many coming and going that the apostles had no time even to eat.
MARK 6:31

Dear Lord, my life is such a hurried, fitful thing! Having only a few short years wherein to live, I seem to rush helter-skelter into action. To be active in the service of my fellow man is much needed, and is my plain duty according to my sphere of life. But always and everywhere there is an equal need that I should "come away" into solitude with You and replenish my soul that it faint not by the way. This lesson I must learn; and when, as in Your life, in mine, too, there are many "coming and going," call my soul into solitude, there to "rest for a while" in Your company.

KEEPING OUR EYES ON CHRIST

Remember Yahweh in that distant country, let Jerusalem be in your mind.

JEREMIAH 51:50

Jesus, my God, that I may remember You always; remember You in the early morning when a new day lies untarnished before me; remember You at high noon, that You may pardon the lapses of the vanished hours and may speed the moments yet to come; remember You at the close of day, when the shadows fall, that You may guard our sleeping and wake us unto another day, be it the radiant day of heaven or another twilight day in the valley of tears. Grant me, Lord Jesus, the grace to remember You when I need You most!

BORROWING FUN

I exult for joy in Yahweh, my soul rejoices in my God.

ISAIAH 61:10

Jesus, dear, there is a lot of fun in life when You are present and I am conscious of Your presence. But when I forget You and try to play the game of life according to my own ways and rules, how blank and dull it becomes! My heart soon tires of it and keeps calling for a change and for new work and new scenes. Stay with me always and let me catch Your smile when You are pleased with me. Let me look within the shell of things and be conscious always of the deep abiding realities of my life and what a happy, joyous thing it is to see it through for You! Just teach me the fun of doing things for God!

ONE IN CHRIST JESUS

There are no more distinctions between Jew and Greek, slave and free, male and female, but all of you are one in Christ Jesus.

GALATIANS 3:28

Dear Lord, I am quite ashamed of myself. There is a lot of bickering; and I myself have been guilty of a lot. I am so pitiably small that I clutch at every chance to appear somewhat important. I want now this job, now that, because it will draw men's eyes to me. I want my own plans for Your work to go through because I like to hear my praises sung. I want my own sweet way at home, at play, at work, no matter what others want. And yet we are all *one* in You, we all form Your Mystical Body and so are members each to each. How unseemly it all is! I am truly sorry, Lord, and with Your grace I shall try to forget myself, that I may merge my littleness into the vastness of Your Mystical Body.

KEPT FOR JESUS CHRIST

From Jude, servant of Jesus Christ and brother of James; to those who are called, to those who are dear to God the Father and kept safe for Jesus Christ.

JUDE 1

Dear Jesus, I am so glad that I am so precious to You that You have taken great pains to guard me as Your own. Never let me forget that, and never let me treat myself as though I were some ordinary, worthless thing. Let me always use the means of grace that You have given me as safeguards, and let me grow prouder and happier each day that I am "kept" for You.

FADED DREAMS

Your old men shall dream dreams, and your young men shall see visions.

JOEL 3:1

O Jesus, dearest Lord, this life of mine amid the shadows of this vale of tears is not an easy thing to plan correctly. I start off well upon some way of life with joy at heart and songs upon my lips, and then when weeks have passed and this tingling happiness is gone, it grows at times so hard to down the thought that maybe all was really nothing but a dream, a vain illusion. Stand hard by me then, and make me realize the lasting worth of all You have taught me, and the abiding value of each saintly way. Jesus, keep me faithful to my promises!

KEEPING THE PAST IN MIND

You must not molest the stranger or oppress him,
for you lived as strangers in the land of Egypt.
EXODUS 22:21

Jesus, dearest Lord, remember that years and years ago You said: "I am the Lord, thy Healer." Heal me then, and cleanse me of all that is displeasing in Your sight. I learn so little from my past. I profit so scantily from experience. I know my own frailty and yet when I see a fellow-struggler fall, I am so prone to lift an accusing finger, so quick to raise a critical voice. Give me grace, then, I beg of You, plentiful grace so that I may always keep fresh the memory that I, too, have been "a stranger in the land of Egypt."

WHEN I'M THROUGH, I'M THROUGH

Forgive us our debts, as we have forgiven those who are in debt to us.

MATTHEW 6:12

Dear Jesus, You touched the sore spot of our human littleness when You taught us to pray as You did. You know how petty and mean and small we are and how prone we are to "hold things in." It is a mean trait and we hate to have others act in the same way toward us. I say the prayer You taught me often each day and I cannot say it honestly unless I forgive and forget. And I do want to say it honestly.

FALL IN LOVE WITH GOD

> But you, my dear friends, must use your most holy faith as your foundation and build on that, praying in the Holy Spirit; keep yourselves within the love of God and wait for the mercy of our Lord Jesus Christ to give you eternal life.
>
> JUDE 1:20, 21

Dear Jesus, even from a selfish standpoint I ought to love You. But selfishness is quite an unworthy motive. I want to love You for Your own sake and because of all You are and all that You have given me. Then, whether sun shines or clouds gather, life will be filled with peace, that peace of Yours which the world cannot give and cannot take away. Dear Lord, grant that I may fall in love with You.

YOU'RE HUNGRY

At that time there was a severe famine.
1 MACCABEES 9:24

Dear Jesus, my soul is often a puzzle to me. It is so restless at times. Some of the pleasures it reaches for I need, and some of them I can rightly have. But they leave me wanting something else. Sometimes, the call of sin is loud and its pleasures are blatant in their appeal. Stand by me then, dear Lord, and make me clearly see that all such earthly foods will always leave me hungry.

GROWTH

Jesus increased in wisdom, in stature, and in favour with God and men.

LUKE 2:52

Jesus, my friend, You know the weakness of my heart and how my love for You is hurt and my courage sometimes spoiled when I see how little I have progressed, and how far unlike Your own dear self I am. The years seem almost wasted and their fruitage small, and it is hard to clasp empty hands that once I thought were filled. Give me, then patience, dearest Lord, patience to stand my own childishness, when long years ago I should have put on man's estate, patience to wait the slow years' unfolding of Your image in my soul. Give me a bit of Your own tireless patience with my yet unfinished childhood.

GIVE US A MAN

> The Word was the true light that enlightens all men; and he was coming into the world. He was in the world that had its being through him, and the world did not know him.
>
> JOHN 1:9-10

Jesus, greatest gift of love to me and to all men, we come to You with faint and timid heart. Oh, we're brave at times and seem to our foolish selves to be quite able to come back home to heaven alone. But not for long. It is only for a few fleeting hours and then we cry again, as Peter did on the Galilean lake, and once again lean heavily on Your arm. Grant, dear Jesus, that it may be ever thus, that we shall always come to You, our strong, true Friend.

HONORED—AND SNUBBED

I have learnt to manage on whatever I have, I know how to be poor and I know how to be rich too, I have been through my initiation and now I am ready for anything anywhere.
PHILIPPIANS 4:11, 12

Dear Lord, no matter whether men praise me or not, I shall try to do Your work as You would have me do it. If men take note of it and are helped by it, I shall accept their praise humbly, knowing that it is from You that I receive the power to help them. And if they take no notice of me or of what I am doing, I shall keep on doing it for You. For before all and above all, it is for You and for You alone that I am doing it.

THE HURT OF SEPARATION

> Yahweh gave, Yahweh has taken back. Blessed be the name of Yahweh.
>
> JOB 1:21

Dear Jesus, try as I may, my heart becomes entwined about the things You have given me. Such love is at times my duty; to deny such love is equally at times my clear obligation. I must be on my guard lest such human affection usurp the place that You alone should have. I want to work for You alone, and to live for You alone. So give me grace to keep my heart for You alone and, if other love must come into my heart, let it always be second to Yours, always be finally in terms of Yours. Then, dear Lord, I shall willingly part with all for You, when You ask and as You ask, and if the hurt is great, I shall come to You to have You touch it healingly with "the tenderness of pierced hands."

LOWLY-MINDEDNESS

Learn from me, for I am gentle and humble in heart, and you will find rest for your souls.
MATTHEW 11:29

Dear Jesus, I hate the task that lies before me, for it means the ruthless sacrificing of all smug self-complacency. Yes, I hate it heartily, until I kneel beside the manger and stand well within the shadow of the cross and find my God an outcast. Then I love it all and long to be done with the plaudits of men, long to arrest the gropings of this fickle heart for human praise. It is all a child's pompous parade and I would fain outgrow my childish years. Let me learn at length a bit of lowly-mindedness!

CONDESCENSION

To Yahweh your God belong indeed heaven and the heaven of heavens, the earth and all it contains; yet it was on your fathers that Yahweh set his heart for love of them, and after them of all the nations chose their descendants, you yourselves up to the present day.

DEUTERONOMY 10:14-16

Jesus, most gracious, most courteous of friends, how little thought You seem to take of all Your high estate! Like every other lover, You forget Yourself and think only to please the one You love, poor me. Heaven with its choirs is Yours, and the skies with the music of its swinging spheres are Yours, and the earth with all its blithe children is Yours, and yet You seem to hold them all as nothing, so that You may win my love. So, coming near, You dwell near my earthly home, so that when the mood comes, I can hasten unto You. Yes, and not merely speak with You but even hold You within myself as my poor heart's guest. O Jesus, never was a friend so kind, so self-forgetful! And yet, I am so forgetful of You. Just give me grace in the future to love You a little more in return, to visit You just a bit more often in return, to receive You just a bit more frequently in return for Your love.

INDISPENSABILITY

When you have done all you have been told to do, say, "We are merely servants: we have done no more than our duty."

LUKE 17:10

Dear Jesus, I am apt to have a distorted sense of my importance.Certainly there is work for which You have deigned to need me and that I must do and I want to do it. But let me not exaggerate my work or think myself indispensable. That is a sad state of mind. I will try, dear Lord, to work hard for You and to do all the good I can for You, realizing all the time that I am by no means indispensable.

JUST TIRED

"My father," he said, "if it is possible let this cup pass me by."
MATTHEW 26:39

"Just tired"—and yet it is quite wrong to yield and betray it by our actions. It is an effort to hold one's tongue and not say unpleasant or angry things. It is just then that we must take our will into our own hands and, with God's grace helping us, do what we think is right, no matter what it costs.

Dear Jesus, You were just tired once and You know exactly how it feels. We get that way often. It isn't that we want to have no trials in life. It isn't that we want to quit or that we don't love You anymore. No, dear Lord, that isn't it, and You know it. So, in our hours of darkness we shall try to kneel beside You in Your agony and gain new strength and courage from Your bravery. Tired Jesus, help us when we get "just tired."

PLAYING OUR OWN PART

Saul was very angry; the incident was not to his liking. "They have given David the tens of thousands," he said, "but me only the thousands."

1 SAMUEL 18:8

Dear Jesus, You know what a jealous person I am. I am always wanting to be otherwise, always grieving because I am not called to play the part in life that others play. It is childish, but it is true, much as it hurts me to admit it. So please let me learn to stop this yearning to play another's part and give me the sense to attend to myself and to my own affairs, the sense to use all my energy to play my own part well.

HURT FEELINGS

A man's shrewdness shows in equanimity, his self-respect in overlooking an offense.
PROVERBS 19:11

Dear Jesus, how much good is spoiled in my own life and in the lives of others by my hurt feelings. I grow peevish and quite out of sorts when others pass me by or merely seem to overlook me, and then my work suffers and perhaps even my health, if my sensitivity reaches undue bounds. It is all a pity, Lord; so help me to get over it! Children fret at everything, but I am supposed to be full-grown. So give me grace to take life as it is and not to give way so frequently to hurt feelings.

THROWN RIGHT UP AGAINST GOD

Unload your burden on to Yahweh, and he will support you; he will never permit the virtuous to falter.

PSALMS 55:22

Dear Lord, I need You as only a creature can need God. For the friends that You have given me I thank You and for my own strength, too. But those fail at times and must finally fail, for as Your handiwork, Your creature, I need *You*. It is, though, hard at times to come to You, to call upon You, to feel that You can and will help. So give me the grace always to have perfect confidence in You, above all then, when I am "thrown right up against God."

SEEKING HELP RIGHTLY

I am thirsty.

JOHN 19:28

Dear Lord, no man can know what Your Real Presence means, save only he who comes and watches daily at Your gates and waits at Your doors. No other comfort is there in this land of tears that approaches it, whether it be a joy or a sorrow that moves our souls. To You I come, to You I tell my heart's own story, from You in ways which You alone could tell I draw fresh courage for life's battles. "For, though I should walk in the midst of the shadow of death I fear no evils, for Thou are with me, Thy rod and Thy staff, they have comforted me."

A CONSTANT VISITOR

Happy the man who listens to me, who day after day watches at my gates to guard the portals.
PROVERBS 8:34

Dear Jesus, I am glad You have taught me that it is well not to keep my load of sorrow to myself and to stumble ahead unaided. I know I must come to You if I am to be really helped and yet I realize that, knowing this poor heart of mine, You will be glad to have me tell my crosses to another pilgrim in the vale of tears, another pilgrim who has learned to carry crosses, too, by looking up and beyond the mists that cloud our vision here to our home above. And I would ask You to send me such a friend always, that my weary and perhaps wavering steps may be led more surely back to You.

AN EPIC OUT OF TWO GRUNTS

What I command you is to love one another.
JOHN 15:17

Dear Jesus, give me a bit of common sense and, more than that, give me a bit of Your own poise. There are many things in life that bring irritation and friction. Others *are* thoughtless and inconsiderate at times, and even unjust. But I would be more mature and more of a Christian if I handled the upsets in a self-controlled way. It's all very clear to me now in the quiet of prayer, but it is not so clear at the moment when things are going wrong. And so I beg You now to give me then, and always, grace enough not to make "an epic out of two grunts."

LORD, IF YOU DON'T COME ACROSS. . . !

The day I called for help you heard me and you increased my strength.

PSALMS 138:3

Dear Lord Jesus, sometimes You make it hard to serve You. At least it seems so to our minds, which can see so little. It is very hard to find that You will not use my best talents or that You will not permit me to work where I am sure I could do most for You. I know You know best but, frankly, it is hard to knuckle down and do things the way You want. So, Lord, give me the grace to accept Your plans willingly at all times, but most of all when you discard what seems to be my best.

"I FELT COWARDLY"

My soul is sorrowful to the point of death. Wait here and keep awake with me.
MATTHEW 26:38-39

Dear Jesus, I am very grateful for the way in which You permitted yourself to feel fear in the Garden of Your Agony. By that, You have taught me that when I begin to feel cowardly in my own life I need not reprove myself; nor will You blame me for it. All You expect of me is to keep on fighting my way to Heaven whether I feel brave or courageous, whether the skies are sunny or clouded. All You want me to do is to come to You for more help when I feel cowardly.

YOU SAID I COULD CALL ON YOU

"Come to me, all you who labour and are overburdened, and I will give you rest."
MATTHEW 11:28

Dear Jesus, what a help it is to know that I have Your "standing invitation" to come to You whenever and wherever I need You. That ought to mean everything to me and it does now as I think it over prayerfully with You. Never let me lose that conviction which is one of the most priceless treasures of my life. In youth or in the middle years or in old age, when I have sinned and when I have broken Your laws, when I have loved You and when I have been mean to You let me always turn to You with the cry: "You said I could call on You."

WHEN DAVID WAS BLUE

More and more are turning against me, more and more rebelling against me, more and more saying about me, "There is no help for him in his God."

PSALMS 3:1, 2

Dear Lord, I get blue at times as everyone does. I get sick and tired of the daily fight of life. I get fed up with its problems and tired-out from its pains. That is why I sometimes just want to be done with it. At times I have quit, but I am sorry now that I played the coward. Please don't let me act that way again. Instead, let me be like David and always remember that You are my protector and the lifter of my head.

WE WERE HOPING!

Our own hope had been that he would be the one to set Israel free.

LUKE 24:21

Dear Lord Jesus, how often have I, too, said "I had hoped"? Life is full of unfulfilled hopes and dead dreams. But they are all minor dreams, lesser hopes. The one hope I have that will never go wrong is to be Your servant and to fulfill Your purpose and do Your will. That hope cannot go wrong if I use the graces You send me. Please help me, then, to do just that.

“IN HIS OWN PERSON HE KILLED THE HOSTILITY”

For he is the peace between us, and has made the two into one. . . . In his own person he killed the hostility.

EPHESIANS 2:14, 17

Dear Jesus, how can I ever justify myself in holding a grudge or, worse still, hating someone? Of course I may be offended. Of course, I may have many supposed reasons for nursing hurt feelings. But if I am Your true follower I can never allow enmity, great or small, to get into my heart. You have killed all that. Never let me bring it to life again.

WHEN OTHERS SEE OUR WEAKNESSES

He took Peter and the two sons of Zebedee with him. And sadness came over him.
MATTHEW 26:37

Dear Lord Jesus, I thank You for the lesson You have taught me by what happened to You in the Garden. It must have been very difficult for You who were God to become so helpless and very disconcerting for You to appear overcome with fear. But You allowed this to happen for my good. So, in my hours of helplessness and fear, let me take it as You did and let me offer up to You the deep humiliation of it all.

JUST WAIT!

Since this vision is for its own time only:
eager for its own fulfillment, it does not deceive;
if it comes slowly, wait,
for come it will, without fail.
HABAKKUK 2:3

Dear Lord Jesus, the world around me presses in on all sides and the trials of life rise up to confront me. Heaven seems awfully far away at times and Your promises quite unreal and, honestly, quite unfulfillable. It is then that I am in danger of chucking it all aside or at least of slowing down in Your service. When the vision does get blurred and seems too far off, just give me grace to know it will eventually appear and will not lie. Give me grace just to wait.

SADNESS NOT FOR MAN

The vine has withered, the fig tree wilts away; pomegranate, and palm, and apple, every tree in the field is drooping. Yes, gladness has faded among the sons of men.

JOEL 1:12

Jesus, Giver of all good gifts, give me the joyousness of Your saints. It means so much to keep Your sunlight in my heart and I am so prone to miss the silver lining of the clouds You send my way. I am a foolish child, without a child's glad heart. But make me a happy-hearted child and keep me so in all the darkness of this life until the morning of Heaven comes and in the morning You will "wipe away all tears from our eyes and death shall be no more, nor mourning, nor crying, nor sorrow shall be any more, for the former things are passed away."

GOD'S STRANGE WAYS

We know that by turning everything to their good God cooperates with all those who love him, with all those that he has called according to his purpose.

ROMANS 8:28

Dear Jesus, life is quite a puzzle to me and at times it stumps me. I just can't make it out and sometimes I cannot make You out either. Yet You love me and have my good at heart. You have Your own way of getting what You want, so let me remember that always, especially when the pieces of the jigsaw puzzle simply don't seem to fit at all.

SEEKING A DOCTOR

The spirit of the Lord Yahweh has been given to me. . . . He has sent me to bring good news to the poor, to bind up hearts that are broken.
ISAIAH 61:1

O Jesus, divine physician of my soul, teach me to come to You that all my ailments may be cured. There are many within my soul and yet I seem to have no desire to be healed. It is strange, is it not, that when my body grows ill I hasten for relief but care hardly at all to have that which is immortal within me brought to perfect health? Teach me to yearn for health of soul; teach me to be really anxious not to lose it; and if at times, dear Lord, I am in failing health and haven't sense enough to ask for help, with a true physician's interest, please force me into ways that will bring back health again.

STANDING IT

Whatever happens to you, accept it, and in the uncertainties of your humble state, be patient.
ECCLESIASTICUS 2:4

Dear Jesus, give me the bravery of sufferance. It is an easy thing to rush into battle when the alarm sounds, to strike lusty blows and win a sudden victory or die a hero's death. But to stand and be still and not to murmur as the trifling crosses of every day come upon me, that is hard. To hold my peace when hour after hour brings fresh irritations, that is hard, Lord Jesus, yet it is my task, the task you have given me and therein will lie my sanctity. So help me to take all that shall be brought upon me and in my sorrow to endure, and in my humiliation to keep patience.

GET ABOVE THE CLOUDS

Will you not give us life again, for your people to rejoice in you? Yahweh, show us your love, grant us your saving help.

PSALMS 84:6

Dear Jesus, disappointment and sorrow are the lot of all mankind. Those who know and love You ought to be able to manage their days of gloom. It's hard—of course it is—and You deigned to allow Yourself to find it hard when You were on earth in the form of a man. But even though it is hard, we must try to handle it. You are always ready to help us. So give us grace at all times in order that we may "get above the clouds."

GOD'S TIRED MAN

Love is strong as Death. . . . Love no flood can quench, no torrents drown.
SONG OF SONGS 8:7, 8

Dear Jesus, I often get tired from doing things that are useless, or at least of no permanent value. That is not always wrong, because life must have its hours of ease and recreation. But I know I could be tired more often from doing things for You and for the souls You love. In the past I have not often been tired for You, and I fear it is because I do not love You as I should. So give me the grace to fall desperately, absorbingly in love with You; then I really will begin to work for You as I should.

HATING TO BE REPROVED

Whoever resents reproof walks in the sinner's footsteps.

ECCLESIASTICUS 21:6, 7

Dear Jesus, that would, indeed, be a sad, sad day when I would resent correction. It is not easy to have another tell me of my faults; and yet I know from all human history and from my own short past that the road of life is filled with pitfalls, when one runs along it without a guide. So please protect me against a self-sufficiency which would wall me off from the advice and correction of others! Until You call me home, let me keep common sense enough not to hate to be reproved. Then I shall not walk, or at least not for long, in the footsteps of a sinner.

A FRIEND IN NEED

So I say to you: Ask, and it will be given to you; search, and you will find; knock, and the door will be opened to you. For the one who asks always receives; the one who searches always finds; the one who knocks will always have the door opened to him.

LUKE 11:9, 10

Jesus, friend of the weary and faint of heart, who can tell what You are to us in hours of loneliness and grief? Life has its joys and we thank You from our hearts for them, for those brief foretastes as they are of eternal bliss. But life has its sorrows, too, sorrows so often unsharable and unshared. To You, then, we come and lay before You the wounds we have received. Jesus, You will help us bear them, You will listen to our oft-told tale, will You not, dear Lord? If you do, will not the joy be Yours, as well as ours, when we, whom You have saved, meet You on the farther shore?

GOD'S LOVERS SMILE

> Go, eat your bread with joy and drink your wine with a glad heart; for what you do God has approved beforehand.
>
> ECCLESIASTES 9:7

Dear Jesus, there should be no gloom in my life if I am really in love with You. I do not put on a long face when I am with a human friend. Then I should not and will not put it on when I am with You. There is no joy like the joy of loving and serving You, and I want all to catch from me the sweet contagion of Your love. As one of Your lovers, let me learn to smile. Teach me to smile through the pleasant hours of life; teach me to smile through life's dark hours; teach me to smile at home and at work; teach me to smile in youth and in old age. And when death comes, let me smile with the assurance that my works have been pleasing to You.

TUCKING THE FUTURE AWAY WITH GOD

Each day has enough trouble of its own.
MATTHEW 6:34

Dear Jesus, You know the weakness of my heart to reach out into the future and worry over what it may bring. It is a foolish thing to borrow trouble when so much is mine already, and worse than that it is not fair and square to You. My past is one long series of protecting acts from Your ever watchful providence and it is not right to feel You will be less kind than You have been. So, dearest Lord, to show my confidence in You, I shall take Your sound advice and let the evil of each day suffice me. I shall leave the days to come alone and here and now I tuck the future away with You.

THE WAY OF LOVE

Where the Spirit of the Lord is, there is freedom.
2 CORINTHIANS 3:18

Dear Jesus, give me a growing sense of this "large liberty of the children of God." I want to serve You out of love and not because I must; and I want to perform each duty of life not because I am obliged, but because I am in love with You. Then will Your service be pleasant as it ought to be, and I shall run along the way of Your commandments with joy, for all that I shall do and all that I omit to do, will find its reason in my love for You and Your love for me.

ME—A SAINT!

Soul of Christ, make a saint of me.

Anima Christi

Can any but omnipotent love find a way to accomplish what seems so hopeless? To the soul of Christ then we must fly for help. It is from the Blessed Sacrament we must gain our strength. With Jesus in our hearts the dross of sinful ways will be burned away; with the sweet whisper of his voice will come our hearkening unto grace, and then we shall become like unto Him, for we shall grow "in age and grace and wisdom before God and man." "Soul of Christ," attempt what seems so hard, attempt to "make a saint of me." My heart is ready, O God, my heart is ready!

HEART-WEARY

Come to me, all you who labour and are overburdened, and I will give you rest.
MATTHEW 11:28

Dear Jesus, You made my heart as it is, and it needs sympathy and understanding. No, I do not want to be petted and coddled, for that is unworthy of one grown up, but I do crave the cheering word, the look of encouragement, the "Well done!" that comes from the heart. I can find this at times from human friends, but sometimes I cannot. But from You I can always find it and it means everything to know that You read me aright and understand and are near to help me and to encourage me. Dear Jesus, just grant me the grace always to come to You, no matter how broken I may be on the wheel of life; for You will not break the bruised reed nor quench the smoking flax, but will always speak the helping word and reach the uplifting hand to those that labor and are heavy-burdened.

A GRAB-BAG SOUL

That is how I run, intent on winning; that is how I fight, not beating the air.

1 CORINTHIANS 9:26

Dear Jesus, I am getting along in years and I really ought to be making something out of myself. I want to, but—! If ever a phrase hit off my soul it is that: a grab-bag soul. I have tried to be good, now this way, now that. I have tried to avoid now this fault, now that. But it has all been a hit-and-miss attempt. So give me grace now to study my soul and to form a definite, abiding plan of self-conquest and self-improvement, and let me stop once and for all this helter-skelter way of acting that makes me have a grab-bag soul.

"BUY AN ICE-BAG"

But he was silent and made no answer at all.
MARK 14:61

Dear Jesus, I have often messed things up in life because I have failed to keep my poise. You know, as well as I do, that life can be very exasperating at times and that others "get on my nerves" dreadfully. It is hard for me to hold myself in then, and very hard not to say and do nasty things. But it just makes matters worse—and life is bad enough at best without my knowingly making it worse. And it is so untrue to all the examples You have given me. So please give me the grace to keep "cool, calm, and collected" all the time, and to keep an ice-bag on my heated brain when the temperature rises too high.

STUBBORN

Bow down, then, before the power of God.
1 PETER 5:6

Dear Jesus, let me always have common sense enough to be convinced that I may easily be mistaken. That is sheer common sense, and it is true humility. I may know many things, and be quite capable to manage much aright. But still I can be wrong; I still can make mistakes. So give me grace never, never to be so stubborn that I refuse reasonable and legitimate advice, but to be ever mindful of my essential liability to make mistakes.

YOU CAN'T BEAT GOD

Who can fathom his magnificent deeds? Who can assess his magnificent strength, and who can go further and tell of his mercies?

ECCLESIASTICUS 18:3-6

Dear Jesus, I am so happy that You are what You are—God without any limit to all You have; without limit to Your kindness, to Your power, to Your justice, to Your love, to Your mercy. Sometimes as a willful child I am displeased with You. I forget all You have done and are doing for me. I am truly sorry that I have ever wronged Your love and forgotten Your mercies. No one can ever equal You in all Your infinite perfections, and I am so glad of that. I am happy that "You can't beat God."

THEY THOUGHT CHRIST DIDN'T CARE

"Master, do you not care? We are going down!"
MARK 4:38

Dear Jesus, I show ingratitude when I doubt Your interest in me. And yet, there are so many times when I doubt. It is not fair to You, not after all You have done for me and all You have told me. I should trust You in big things and in little things. In everything. And I want to. So please help me never again even for a moment to harbor the thought that You do not care.

HE SHOOK THE WORLD FROM A PRISON

> I am glad to tell you, brothers, that the things that happened to me have actually been a help to the Good News. My chains, in Christ, have become famous not only all over the Praetorium but everywhere, and most of the brothers have taken courage in the Lord from those chains of mine and are getting more and more daring in announcing the Message without any fear.
>
> PHILIPPIANS 1:12-13

Dear Jesus, it does seem perfectly useless at times to try to do anything for You or for anybody else. And You know how easy it is for me to get discouraged then and to quit. St. Paul must have felt that way in prison, but by Your grace he kept on trying, and look at the marvels he wrought. So please give me Your strong grace never to give up trying, never to grow sour and bitter and, above all, never to quit no matter where I am, no matter how hampered I may seem to be.

BE MINDFUL OF MY BONDS

Here is a greeting in my own handwriting—PAUL. Remember the chains I wear. Grace be with you.

COLOSSIANS 4:18

Jesus, ransomer of our souls, "if we have forgotten the name of God, and if we have stretched forth our hands to a strange God, shall not God search out these things?" Oh, what a search You would have to make, then, of the past! Days and weeks and months we have set up strange, petty idols in our hearts and made slaves again of the souls You had redeemed. But, Jesus dear, this must not be again and with Your helping grace it will not be again. Come failure or come success, come joy or sorrow, we will ever hearken to Your voice: "Remember the chains I wear."

A KNOW-IT-ALL

Doubtless, you are the voice of the people, and
when you die, wisdom will die with you!
JOB 12:2

Dear Lord, as life advances we ought to absorb experiences and so grow more fit to take place in the adult world with its larger problems. Yet, there is a danger that our heads will be turned and that we will become unduly willing to pronounce on everything. So give us the double grace to grow and at the same time to cherish always a reticence that springs from true humility. Give me a sense of humor and much patience, and then I shall reach a higher place in Heaven. And, for myself, please never let me become a know-it-all.

HUMDRUM-NESS

He went down with them and came to Nazareth and lived under their authority.

LUKE 2:51

Dear Jesus, You were good enough to lead a very humdrum, uneventful life so as to match Your life with ours in what most of us find hardest. It was very thoughtful of You to do this, for it makes the beaten track of everyday life so much easier and it gives me more courage to tackle the same old tasks day in and day out. Just give me grace to become holier and holier through the very humdrumness of life.

ONE WITH GOD, A MAJORITY

With God on our side who can be against us?
ROMANS 8:31

Dear Jesus, there is so much opposition to good in this world that often all of us feel like giving up. You know how hard I try at times to serve You and to keep others in Your service or to win still others to Your love. Yet so often, very often, I have every reason to believe that my efforts are doomed to failure. And so, dear Lord, whatever I plan to do, and whatever I undertake for good, just let me remember to call You in, to take You into partnership. Let me not be worried over the outcome, let me not grow anxious when the dice of life are loaded, but let my confidence be firm; for one with You, my God, is a majority, and we are bound to win.

MIDAS-TOUCH

Laying his hands on each he cured them.
LUKE 4:41

Jesus, in childhood days, I read of the fabled king whose touch turned all into gold and in the daydreaming of those years I quite envied him his gift, but I felt sure it never could come true. Yet when years have passed, I find there is a truer, higher Midas-touch in life, and that You alone possess it. How kind of You to make my dreams come true! Teach me, dearest Lord, to bring all I have to You that You may touch it all, joy and sorrow alike, love and fear, sunshine and rain, life and death. Then and then only will the fairy tales of childhood have come true.

I bring you news of great joy, a joy to be shared by the whole people. Today in the town of David a savior has been born to you; he is Christ the Lord.

LUKE 2:10, 11

Dear infant Savior, with the humble shepherds, I kneel by the crib a yet unredeemed world has given You. Your handiwork has indeed been spoiled when men could treat an infant, an infant-God, like this. Homeless, You lie before me; but, Jesus, be homeless no longer! Poor though it be, come make my heart Your home. You ask for it; so let it be. Take possession of my heart, strange dwelling as it is for God, and make it Yours forever. Make it all Your own so that none may share therein a part. From early morn, all through the long hours of the day until the shadows fall, come stay with me, Lord Jesus.

INVITATIONS

Now when the angels had gone from them into heaven, the shepherds said to one another, "Let us go to Bethlehem and see the thing that has happened."

LUKE 2:15

O Jesus, as of old on Bethlehem's starlit hill the words of pressing welcome sounded, so may they ever hang upon my lips! Thus were the simple shepherds brought unto You over hill and dale when first You came and dwelt among us. Thus it was that they won Your grace and Mother Mary's smile and Holy Joseph's kindly courtesy. Thus, too, today may I bring fellow-exiles, all footsore and hungry, unto You that You may draw us nearer unto You. Teach me, Jesus, welcomer of souls, to extend to all Your earnest, constant welcome.

THE MAGI-QUEST

We saw his star as it rose and have come to do him homage.

MATTHEW 2:2

Dear Jesus, king of my heart, may I never be slothful in hearkening to Your call! It would be a shameful thing where I to falter and be loath to come, for I have known these many years the joy of heeding Your invitation. At times I know I have been rude and have turned away, and at other times I dragged slothful feet to tasks You held before me. Oh, let this never be again, but Magi-like let me always come most willingly, most gladly, when You call.

TIME FLIES

My tent is pulled up, and thrown away like the tent of a shepherd.

ISAIAH 28:12

The past is over and gone and Christ Jesus stands side by side with us to begin our New Year. "Fear not; it is I. Yes, strange, incomprehensible though it may seem, I am with you still though you have offended Me so often. Let bygones be bygones! All I ask of you is a future different from the past. Yes, even less than this. All I ask of you *now* is the strong will, the hearty resolve to rise with Me and to hold fast to My hand during the days and weeks and months of the coming year, lest you stray once more from My side. From out of the crib before which you kneel these days I stretch My tiny hands, asking this one gift of you. Strange heart of man, to all others you will give a Christmas gift; will you refuse Me Mine?"

> They pressed him to stay with them. "It is nearly evening," they said, "and the day is almost over."
>
> LUKE 24:29

Stay with us, dear Lord Jesus, it is growing dusk. The twilight of oncoming desolation, of gathering sorrows, of rooted pain, from which the heart may wish us freed of "dull and doomed regrets," is already upon us. Like little children, we are afraid of the dark. Like little children we come to You. We do not ask that the chalice of Your sending be taken away; we do not even ask for light. We only ask for You to stay with us, only ask that we may hear Your voice over the sunless waters that reach into our very soul: "Be of good heart; it is I, fear ye not." Stay with us, Your faint-hearted, timid children, dear Lord, until the mist is lifted and daylight has routed the distorted shadows of our soul's night.

SAY SOMETHING THAT WILL HELP

My eyes turn to the heights, take care of me, be my safeguard.

ISAIAH 38:14

Dear Jesus, sometimes, You know, my heart is so numbed with pain and anguish it cannot pray. Sometimes the crosses of life seem thrust too full upon me and bear me down too mercilessly. Sometimes, in otherwise, the world with its pleasures is quite too attractive and bewitches my silly heart, so that it would fain stray from You. O Jesus, in those hours let me always run to You, and let me always cry to You—as once a soul did to Your priest: "Lord, say something that will help me." And Jesus dear, please always say that something.

FOOD OF THE BRAVE

I have food to eat that you do not know about.
JOHN 4:32

"I have food to eat that you do not know about," O world, and cannot know, and that is why my heart is strong. That is why I can bear the smart of pain, the shock of shattered nerves, the agony of bruised and battered limbs, with a playful word upon my shrunken lips; that is why poverty has no sting and riches no siren call; that is why I can kneel beside the bed of dying loved ones and with trembling fingers close their eyes in sleep that knows no waking, and yet go back to life with the same old smile of joy; that is why, when Christ, my Captain, calls, I can leave the world and turn my back upon its fleeting baubles and bind my life with triple vow to serve my King.

NOTHING TO LIVE FOR

> We teach what scripture calls the things that no eye has seen and no ear has heard, things beyond the mind of man, all that God has prepared for those who love him.
>
> 1 CORINTHIANS 2:9

Dear Jesus, how can we thank You for making the struggle that is life worthwhile? It is hard, at times very hard, to keep on plodding ahead when everything is against us. If the grave is the end, then the young suicide was right. But, thanks to Your grace, we know it is not the end but only the beginning of a glorious life forever. So, thanks again for making life worthwhile—and never permit us to forget that it is.

EVEN TO MY OLD AGE

In your old age I shall be still the same, when your hair is grey I shall still support you. I have already done so, I have carried you, I shall support and deliver you.

ISAIAH 46:4

Friend of my younger days, Friend of my maturing years, Friend, too, when life shall ebb into eternity, constant and unswerving in Your love for me, I kneel here to thank You for Your friendship. You alone know what it means to me; what it means to realize there is no sorrow I need hold back from You, no meanness, no cowardice I need hide from You lest Your shoulder bear not the burden and Your heart be not brave enough to love me still. What it means to know that my coming can never be ill-timed! Lord Jesus, I am contented now and my weary heart has found its rest. "Lover of souls, great God, I look to thee."

OUR LORD EXPECTS US

> I am going now to prepare a place for you, and after I have gone and prepared you a place, I shall return to take you with me.
>
> JOHN 14:3

O Jesus, from all eternity You have loved me with a love such as only God can have. From all eternity You have planned to have me bring my soul to You beautiful with all the luster of Your many graces. How can I disappoint You, my God? No, it must not be, dear Lord; it must not be. Give me but Your grace; give me but the strength to profit by Your grace. Then when I hasten home, my Jesus, You will find me the saint You yearned that I should be.

DAYS OF PREPARATION

After I have gone and prepared you a place, I shall return to take you with me.

JOHN 14:3

O Jesus, "hope of Israel," and my hope, too, let not my life, cheated of its end, retell the story of Your fickle folk. Rather, let the days of my waiting be days of preparation, too—but not alone. No, I must think and pray and talk with You in the sacrament of Your love. Then when the gates of death are swung ajar and I pass within to see You, oh, the joy of that first meeting face to face! The Advent of life will be over and Christmas day will then be here.

"DIED IN HIS SLEEP"

"The time" has come: you must wake up now.
ROMANS 13:11

Dear Jesus, You have generously given me the vision of faith. I have seen beyond the things of sense and time and touched the things of eternity. But that vision becomes tarnished at times and I go about my daily tasks only half-awake to it. That must not be, dear Lord. My time is short and I have much to do. Please grant me the grace that when death comes, be it today or tomorrow, I may not "die in my sleep."

CHRIST STANDS GUARD

May the body of our Lord Jesus Christ be sentinel over your soul unto life everlasting.
Priest's Prayer at Communion

Stand sentinel over us in "our failing years when our strength shall fade," when the call to battle will be the call to join the host of those who have "preceded us in the sign of faith and sleep in the sleep of peace." That will be our last stand; and may we die, Lord Jesus, beneath Your banner, fighting for the souls You have redeemed.

TAKEN NOTICE OF

Well done, good and faithful servant.
MATTHEW 25:21

Jesus, my God, I do so want someone to notice all my ways, and yet I dare not ease this craving by the quest of the praise of men. That would not be right nor can it ease my heart. And so I look to You. As You love my soul, do ever let me realize that You are taking note of all I think or say or do, whether sunshine dances all about my path or hours come that leave scars upon my soul. But most of all when the curtain is drawing across my little stage and my departure is at hand, let me hear Your final praise: "Well done!"

FRIENDLY VISITS

Rabbi—which means teacher—where do you live? Come and see.

JOHN 1:28, 39

Jesus, how completely happy I am in Your dear friendship! The dreaded parting with other friends comes at length, but between us two there neither is, nor will be, any separation. In the heyday of life's powers I come to visit You, and when the twilight comes gathering on, it is You who call me. Thus we shall travel through the years in truest friendship until, dear Jesus, in Your love, You come to call me home.

AMEN.